Find Your Flow Publishing

Copyright © 2016 by Find Your Flow Publishing
All rights reserved.

This book or any portion thereof
may not be reproduced or used in any manner whatsoever
without the express written permission of the publisher
except for the use of brief quotations in a book review.

Printed in the United States of America

First Printing, 2016

Find Your FlowTM
San Diego, CA

www.FindYourFlow.com

The Most Flowing FREE Gift Ever

Go to www.FindYourFlow.com/3steps to access my on some of my best secrets to getting into FLOW. I'll send the "3 Steps to Flow" Mini-Course for FREE straight to your inbox!

After going through these Insider Tips, you'll feel 100% CONFIDENT about how to do it right. You'll be happier, get into flow quicker and avoid getting stuck in ruts.

You'll Discover:

1) Secrets to happiness

(Everybody wants to be happy, but for many people it seems so elusive. The secret to happiness has little to do with the things you have or the money in your bank account. You'll learn how to be happier in the moment and over the long run.)

2) The top 5 case studies

(You probably do at least one of these things everyday! See exactly how to apply this simple process to your life.)

3) Behind the scenes of creating a perfect work day and perfect day of fun

(I'll share with you the one weird trick I used to find my soulmate, create the career that I'm passionate about, and the life of my dreams.)

4) Three unique ideas to try so that you can start to feel tingly happy sensations of flow and joy

(Most people want to get into flow and experience more "good luck" and meet the "right person" or be "in the right place at the right time."

I'll share with you three ideas to transform your life into one that is more fun and flowing!)

5) **The 4 PRACTICAL benefits of getting into flow that you probably haven't thought of yet**

(This is insider knowledge coming from a master flower, not a "guru")

Go to www.FindYourFlow.com/3steps to get the FREE "3 Steps To Flow" Mini-Course!

Table of Contents

The Most Flowing FREE Gift Ever 3

Introduction by Winston Widdes 6

Contact Improv Evolution By Flow Ananda Elaena 8

Sammi "No Pants Sammi" Johnson Ranked #3 in the World - Powerlifting 13

Ashley Ludlow Singer, Songwriter 18

Clinton A. Young Speaker, Author, "The Millennial Mentor" 28

Interview with Jules Schroeder, Founder of CreateU 36

In Conclusion 48

Introduction

by Winston Widdes

Glad you picked up this book! This is the second book in the Social Flower Expert Series!

In this episode we have all new authors sharing their unique experiences with flow. We even have an amazing author, speaker and facilitator who goes by the name, "Flow!" Flow shares her first experience with improvisational contact dancing and how it changed her life. I had never heard of it before meeting her, but I could definitely relate. Many of the elements sound a lot like jiu-jitsu, which I am deeply in love with.

Then, we have an inspirational story from the one and only "No Pants Sammi." She is ranked #3 in the world of Powerlifting (for her weight class). She shares her story about how she got started in the powerlifting sport and how she found her flow doing the impossible and coaching her students to do the same.

Ashley is a singer-songwriter who dives deep into the pain she had experienced when she lost a close friend. She goes on to share an experience as a young girl that triggered a negative body image. Now as she has learned ways to overcome those negative views she is bringing her message to young women (and the world) that you are perfect the way you are!

My good friend Clinton is one of those guys who plays big. Or at least he used to. Until he made a big mistake that cost him almost everything. Then, he was afraid to play at all. He was in a downward spiral. But...he rallied. He has been finding his flow and redirecting into an upward spiral and he is taking his skills to millennials, specifically college students who are about to enter the "real world." His story is one that can help pull you out of a slump and get you going up and up.

I recently did a podcast interview with a fellow music artist and entrepreneur named Jules Schroeder. It was so fascinating that I had to include it in this episode. She recently had a near-death experience and it shifted her whole direction in life. Her story is truly fascinating.

Contact Improv Evolution

By Flow Ananda Elaena

The first time I ever went to a Contact Improv class, I cried.

Not just a few tears. Deep, painful, cathartic sobbing. It started a few moments after I walked in the door. Luckily my boyfriend at the time was there with me and he was great at holding space for me. He took me to another room and my sobs got louder and harder. He held me while I cried and cried.

So many memories from my past came up. Memories of feeling anxious and awkward in school whenever we had to pick partners, feeling lonely and isolated at summer camp, that time when my friends hid from me and didn't want to play with me, the time in preschool when the boys were playing Ninja Turtles and told me I had to be the bad guy, Shredder, feeling like I would never truly be able to get close to people, feeling like I didn't belong, and on and on.

Contact Improvisation Dance (Contact Improv) is partner dancing with no set steps, based on the physics and energy of bodies moving together. It is completely improvised, though there are techniques and a few rules of engagement. For me, it was terrifying and confronting to walk into a room full of strangers, instantly pair up and get so close physically and energetically. That first day, it felt impossible. Eventually though, after about half an hour of emotional releasing, I stopped crying, blew my nose, wiped my eyes, and walked back in the room. By that time there were only a few minutes left. My boyfriend went in and started dancing with someone that he knew. I sat against the wall in a huddled ball and watched.

What I saw was amazing. I watched two experienced dancers flow together in a completely seamless union. One move effortlessly led into the next. Their eyes met, their hearts were open, they communicated so much without saying anything. It was completely improvised and completely mesmerizing. I thought, "I will never be able to do that."

And the next thought was, "I REALLY REALLY want to be able to do that."

I took a break from Contact Improv for a while after that first experience to process what had come up for me. It was fear of connection, feelings of inadequacy, avoidance of intimacy, awkwardness, not wanting to mess up, feeling so stuck in my head, fear of letting people in, fear of being rejected.

To be able to move seamlessly with another in an improvised partner dance takes an incredible amount of openness, vulnerability, sensitivity and presence. You have to be able to really feel someone else, physically, energetically and emotionally, and let them feel you that deeply as well. Those were all things I wanted to cultivate in my life, yet it felt nearly impossible. But something in me knew I had to do it. The immensity of emotion I felt well up instantly when I walked in that room showed me that this was not just a dance form, this was a powerful transformational practice, and I had to keep doing it.

So eventually, after some time, I returned to Contact Improv and kept trying. I kept going. It was still uncomfortable and confronting, but never as dramatic as that first time. In the cathartic experience of my first class, I had popped the bubble around my heart and soul that had kept me from true intimacy for most of my life, and even though I was still like a baby deer with wobbly legs, I kept trying.

With practice, it got easier. I kept being willing to mess up, to accidentally bump elbows or heads, to feel awkward, to confront my shyness. And, it worked. I became better and better.

Not only did I get better at Contact Improv, I got better at life. The dance form was a microcosm of the rest of my life experience. As I allowed more intimacy, openness, sensitivity and vulnerability in my dance, I also began to allow those things more into my other interactions. The intense social anxiety that I used to feel lessened, I was able to let people in more, I gained many more and deeper friendships, I allowed myself to be vulnerable and seen in all aspects of myself, not just the pretty parts, I was less in my head and more in my body and my heart and I became more intuitive and creative.

Through this dance practice I also learned how to open deeply into the Flow State, which forever changed my life. I became able to drop into an improvisational space at will, in dance, in my music and in life and conversations. I truly learned how to "go with the Flow," and fully embody my name. Now when I introduce myself as Flow, most people say something like, "OF COURSE you are!" Or, "That is the perfect name for you!" And, it's true!

Now, 6 years later, I have little to no social anxiety. I have remarkable intuition and experience increased serendipities in life. I am an improvisational musician, an incredibly skillful improvisational dancer, both solo and with partners, and, I teach Contact Improv professionally.

But, the way I teach, I don't just throw people into a class together and expect them to feel comfortable dancing and being that intimate right away. The classes that I teach I call Contact Improv Evolution, because, from my personal and very real experience, this is so much more than a dance. It is truly an evolutionary practice.

When I teach Contact Improv, I first bring everyone into a circle and open up a space of verbal and emotional sharing and intimacy, so they can feel more comfortable with each other and feel safe being seen. Then, I incorporate other trust building, intimacy and vulnerability activities to deepen the group synergy, help everyone drop out of their heads and into their bodies, and familiarize the group with the concepts of energetic sensitivity, awareness and embodied "listening."

From there I start the dance class and I have found that this is a profoundly effective way of accelerated learning and evolution for my students. I cannot fully describe the beauty that I witness every time I teach a class. I watch a group of separate individuals who are slightly nervous, blossom, unfold, soften, connect and open with each other in ways they probably never would have otherwise, in a short period of 1-3 hours. It is remarkable and incredible. We usually end up in a huge group hug and don't want to let go!

People have reported that classes with me have honestly changed their lives. One man said that a 3 hour class with me was equivalent to a year of therapy in how profoundly it impacted him and changed his perspective on himself and reality.

For this reason, I am so grateful for my somewhat traumatic introduction to Contact Improv. It allowed me to really understand that this is an incredibly transformational practice, and develop a way to teach it that addresses the potentially confronting and uncomfortable parts of it with a space of deep unconditional love, acceptance and compassion. While I still have much to learn, and view this as a lifelong practice and journey, I am proud to say that I am now considered an expert in this field and am blessed with the ability and willingness to hold this deep and powerful space for others to go on their own journey into moving through their blocks to intimacy and vulnerability, helping them drop out of their heads and into their bodies, cultivate more energetic sensitivity and intuition, increase self-confidence on and off the dance floor and access the Flow State through Contact Improvisation.

Without this practice, my life and art would not be what they are. I would probably still be very anxious, closed-hearted and often stuck in my head. Contact Improvisation has allowed me to become more embodied, empathic, intuitive, creative and really let people in.

I also have had some of the most profound and transcendental experiences in Contact Improv dances. Together we enter a space where there are no wrong moves. Each movement, each point of contact, is perfectly placed, perfectly aligned with absolutely no effort. We are no longer separate beings, we are no longer trying to do anything. We let go and are moved by creation. With each movement we access more and more pleasure, more sensation, more energy, more ecstasy, more release, healing and opening places within us that we didn't even know were stuck. It's like a cosmic massage that goes so much deeper than the physical. It becomes an experience of perfect union with each other, with the world, with the Universe. It is soul changing and awe inspiring. That is why I do it, why I teach it: for those moments and to inspire and share that type of full surrender, full trust and full Flow with others and with life.

I am so grateful for this practice for so many reasons. It has totally changed my life and opened me to a much broader awareness of what is possible in these bodies, in connection and in life. I know that I will keep doing and teaching it for the rest of my life. It is the most effective way I have discovered to cultivate and enter a state of Flow, and that is when I feel most like myself. Contact Improv has been the most valuable discovery and commitment I have ever made, and now I am committed to bringing this magic, healing, transformation and embodied wisdom to as many people as I can.

Sammi "No Pants Sammi" Johnson
Ranked #3 in the World - Powerlifting

So how do you find your life flow? How about try having multiple jobs in multiple different industries moving to multiple different states until you figure out that working for other people just isn't for you.

I've had about every job you can think of from serving pizza, to filing invoices, to staffing coordinator, to basketball coach, to librarian and that's just to name a few. Every job I had I became bored very easily, would no longer enjoy what I was doing and be ready to move on to the next thing. I always felt I was meant for so much more, I just didn't know what that more was…yet.

After some fortunate life events, I don't say misfortunate because it ultimately led me to where I am now, I moved back to Nevada to be closer to my family in my time of healing. After working a few different jobs that I ended up not enjoying at all, I started working at a gym in December of 2011. During that time I started personal training and training for a bikini competition and that's when I fell in love with lifting heavy and helping people achieve their goals. During this time I was training my personal clients in multiple different styles, allowing me to see how they responded and what worked best for them. Though I gained a great amount of knowledge, all my clients were on different paths and I was starting to realize I enjoyed training my weightlifting clients more than my cardio based clients.

About a year and a half of working at the gym I was ready to leave the small town life and get back to a bigger city. Since I knew I loved the fitness industry I sought out a marketing position with a supplement company in San Jose, CA. I mean what could be better than being right in the mix of the industry you were so passionate about? So I put personal training to the side and thought this was finally my dream career and not just another job. In the process of working for this company for close to two years I saw so many things that turned me off to the fitness industry and it turned out to be nothing as I thought. As for my dream career, it turned out to be more like a nightmare. I went from being in a gym working with people on a daily basis to sitting at a desk 9-10 hours a day and it made me miserable!

I started applying to jobs shortly after my one year mark and in the following 6 months I applied to close to 200 jobs with no regard to what the particular positions were. All I thought about was that I would be so much happier if I was just in a place where I was making more money and wasn't as stressed. I didn't get one interview. I'm not some Joe Schmoe with nothing to offer a company, I have an MBA and plenty of experience to back it up. I was so frustrated at the situation wondering how much longer I could take working for this company because I was near my breaking point.

I had to sit myself down one day and really think about what I wanted to do and what was going to make me happy. There was a reason none of these jobs were happening for me, the universe was trying to tell me something and all I needed to do was listen. I needed to stop fighting the flow of my life. I started thinking about all the different jobs I've had and knew that being in the gym was when I was the most fulfilled. I had a friend who knew a gym owner in a town about an hour away who was looking for a Director of Personal Training and asked if I would be interested. I turned it down not wanting to move, so I applied to a few different positions in San Jose at various gyms and again, nothing. My next life path was sitting in front of me patiently waiting for me to realize it. I reached out to my friend inquiring if the position was still available and it was. After a few interviews I put in my two weeks with the supplement company and started this new chapter of my life.

In February of 2015 I moved and started working. I loved everything about the gym, the job, the people and most importantly I was able to start personal training again. During the time I was working in San Jose I started competing in powerlifting but did not want to force that on any of my clients so I allowed their goals to dictate the workout style. I started to repeat the same process I did in Nevada of finding more excitement in training my lifting clients than my cardio based clients. I never want a client to feel as though I don't care about their progress or check out when I am training them so I made the decision to transition all my clients over to weightlifting. Within a matter a days I felt more at ease and in tune with them and the results they had justified I made the right decision.

Everything seemed to be moving along great, or so I thought. In November I left for a powerlifting competition and when I returned the next week my boss sat me down and basically told me that it didn't make sense for them to pay my salary anymore and the end of the month would be my last paycheck. To say I freaked out inside is an understatement, I panicked. What in the heck am I going to do because in two weeks I will lose 2/3rds of my income! I reached out to every contact I could think of in the area and generated 5 job offers in 4 days.

The next day I had a meeting with one of my mentors, I told him what was going on and that I didn't know what to do. I told him about each opportunity, how I felt about it and started to justify taking the non-fitness related job where I would be making more money but having to commute. He stopped me mid sentence and asked me if money didn't exist what would you do. Well when you put it like that it's easy, I would start my own online coaching business, focus on building my in-person clientele to powerlifters only at his gym and continue spreading my knowledge and passion on the physical and mental benefits of powerlifting. At that point I had to decide if I would fall back into the rat race or take the leap of faith and investment in myself. I chose myself. I knew how hard I worked for others and knew it was time for me to put all that energy into building my own business and see what I was truly capable of. So we sat and talked about what needed to be done to make this successful and at that moment I knew I was making the right decision for my life.

After that conversation, without even marketing myself, I started getting inquiries from women about how I got started in powerlifting and most were interested in having me coach them. I started building my team from that and marketing myself on social media to bring in more potential clients. My business flourished! In January of 2016, I started a Women's Strength Camp which I run out of Athletik Performance Studio in Elk Grove, CA that is for women who have either never touched a weight or are very new to weightlifting. I teach them how to lift and debunk every negative preconceived notion they've ever had about lifting heavy. Of course it is amazing to see them get stronger but more importantly to me is seeing their mental progression and their self-confidence skyrocket. No matter what kind of day I've had or mood I'm in, the minute I start coaching I am instantly at peace and this is how I know I am exactly where I am supposed to be.

Most of us have life cycles that we continually rotate through whether it is our career, friendships, relationships, etc. It is up to you to recognize and break those life cycles and see what can happen when you truly are committed to reaching your goals and accomplishing in life what will make you the most fulfilled. You have to put out what you want, allow the universe to manifest it and be ready to seize the opportunity when you are ready! Always remember you'll never be great at anything if you are trying to be good at everything.

I have gone through my life giving every job, friendship, and relationship 100% and having no regrets. When you live your life that way you will never wonder "what if?" Ensuring that you will never go back to something that is not exactly what you want. Though those times in life may be extremely challenging, it is important to understanding everything you go through leads you to where you're meant to be and will ultimately make you a more evolved person. I definitely didn't take the most direct route but as my dad has always said, "It builds character!"

Ashley Ludlow

Singer, Songwriter

Have you ever felt worthless? Curl-up-in-a-ball, can't-leave-the-house, hot-mess kind of worthless?

Ever asked yourself, "what does anyone see in me?"

"When will I ever be good enough?" or "Why am I here?" I have. I've cried so hard that I can't breathe through my own mucus. Not too long ago, I had what I consider to be a "mental breakdown". I decided to record the audio on my phone so that I could listen to it later when I was of sound mind. Do you know what happened when I listened back? It was hard to hear myself cry. All the things I said were still true for me. But, I was stronger. It didn't make me feel angry or upset. It made me feel glad that I knew in the moment that THAT particular moment would end. That I would live on to see love, laughter, and happy times. I would get to meet new friends and experience different parts of the country and even the world. I would still get bedtime hugs and kisses from my cute kids. In the moment of my mental breakdown, I had enough foresight to see that. But it isn't always that way.

Don't you wish that in your darkest hour you could see the light at the end of the tunnel?

I have a friend named Hannah. We met when she was 14. We were in Rogers and Hammerstein's Cinderella together at a community theater, and we were both ballroom dancers. She is one of the coolest people I know, and I am more than 11 years older than her. She always has a smile on her face. She is the best at pranking people. She is one of those people who just seems to be good at everything. A few months after closing night of the musical, my husband came home from a year long unaccompanied tour of duty and we were stationed about 14 hours away from where Hannah lived. We stayed in touch on Facebook but it wasn't the same. You know how it is.

I remember scrolling through Facebook one day and glancing down to see something her mom posted. Hannah had been in a car accident. The good news? Hannah survived the accident. The bad news was that Hannah had developed a TBI (traumatic brain injury). Her mom said she never was the same after the accident. Hannah took her own life at 16 years old. She couldn't escape her own pain. She couldn't see the light at the end of the tunnel.

If you take one thing from this, and one thing only, I want you to know that there IS a light at the end of the tunnel. You might not be able to see it, but it's there. It might not appear today or tomorrow, or even in a year from now, but sooner or later you'll come out of the tunnel and thank your lucky stars that you didn't give up in the dark. When you wake up next to someone you love, when you're surrounded by people who love you, when you travel to that place you've always wanted to visit, when you meet that lifelong friend, you'll be so happy that you decided to hang in there.

Because, you are irreplaceable. Hannah is irreplaceable. She didn't understand the crater she left down here. The trauma. The pain. The tears. The sadness. The memories. She may have felt like she was misunderstood, like she was a burden, like no one cared about her, but she was so special to so many people. Irreplaceable.

I started writing a song a few years ago and left it when I couldn't find the words to finish. Last year I finished and recorded the song. It's called "Beautiful Soul." In it I talk about Hannah and two other women that made a big impact in my life. Each one of these women didn't seem to understand how completely irreplaceable they were.

Why don't you know you are beautiful? I'm not just talking to women, and I'm not just talking about outer beauty either. Do you know you're a beautiful soul? Do you know you're irreplaceable? There's a way to tell if someone doesn't know. You know what you do? Pay them a compliment. Watch how they respond. You might get an eye roll. You might get a "whatever" or a "yeah right". You might get an over the top, enthusiastic "YES I AM!" There are dozens of other responses like these that can help you recognize if someone doesn't know how amazing they are. I'm going to teach you a way to start claiming your awesomeness. It's such a well-kept secret that hardly anyone uses it anymore. Are you listening? Here it is: When someone pays you a compliment, say, "thank you."

Try to stop yourself from minimizing it. Not "Oh you're funny, but thank you" or "Are you sure? Thanks, I guess." I want to hear a confident and resounding, "Thank you." Then see how many seconds of awkward silence follow. But seriously! How many times do you blow off compliments? Someone says something nice. You don't have the confidence to know if it's true or not, so you figure you'll play it safe just in case they're joking and all will be well in social land.

Have you ever tried giving someone a compliment and they just won't take it? Isn't it frustrating? You'll overhear a conversation like this one in the halls of any high school:

"I love your hair like that!"
"Really? I seriously didn't even brush it."
"No way! You look so good!"
"It's SO gross! Don't even look at me right now."
"No, I'm serious! It's so cute!"
"Please, just stop. Not even!"
"But I..."
"N..."
"But wait..."

"St..."
"But…"
"Whatever!"

This is s a bit of an exaggeration, but have you experienced something similar? How does that make you feel when you're the one trying to give a genuine compliment?

Sad? Frustrated? Angry? Embarrassed? Think about that when you receive a compliment next time and instead, say "Thank you."

Do you remember worrying about this when you were a young kid? I remember feeling free. I remember being uninhibited. I sometimes wish I could go back for a day just to remember what it was like to be 5 or 6 again. Back before everything got complicated. Back before I was so worried about what I looked like, who was popular, or how much money I made. Earlier, I told you that I wasn't just talking about physical beauty, but that is a huge part of this conversation. Body image plays a big role in how we see ourselves as a whole.

I have struggled with my body image for a long time. Just a few years ago I was headed home from a long road trip with my family. It was late and the kids had fallen asleep in the back, so I was talking with my husband about some deep seeded self-worth issues. I remember feeling particularly discouraged. I just didn't understand why I had to work so hard just to maintain my weight when the friend I had visited had trouble keeping weight on. I was tearing and my husband was trying to console me. He started asking me questions like: When was the first time you felt bad about your body? I thought for a while. I thought of how much I loved dance class up until I started comparing myself to the other girls. I remember having a school assignment that required me to weigh myself. I was 11 years old and weighed 115lbs. I remember feeling disappointed by the number, but I couldn't remember why I felt that way. What other number did I have to compare with it?

Then, I remembered something. It was something that I had hidden away in my memory because I didn't like to think about it. When I was at least 8 years old I got invited to a sleepover at my friend's house. She lived kiddy corner across the street and I was so excited that my mom let me go. I remember they had a VHS player and rollercoaster POV tape that had 3D glasses that came with it. (If it sounds like I'm speaking Greek, it's because I'm old.) Basically we could watch a video from the perspective of someone riding a roller coaster. The 3D glasses made it pop out of the TV screen. Then, I remember hearing snickering. I turned around and a few girls were gathered around an open magazine. One of the girls told us she had found it under the couch. I walked over as my curiosity peaked. The magazine read "Playboy" across the front. I'd never seen or heard of that one. At that point all the girls were gathered around the couch. There on the page was a pornographic image that I've never been able to fully erase from my memory. She turned over a few pages. I stared wide-eyed as I examined the page. I remember one of the girls felt bad and walked away. To this day I wish I had walked out with her.

I feel very blessed because for as long as I can remember I've had a safe relationship with my parents. When I returned home from that party, I told them what had happened. They were able to teach me what it was I saw and warn me about avoiding it at all costs.

So there I was, reliving this memory in the car. My husband was there with me quietly listening through my sobs of shame and sadness. My sadness turned to anger. What kind of a father would keep a pornographic magazine under the couch in a room where his daughter and her friends would be having a sleepover? My anger then turned from the dad to the media. Why is anyone okay with this, this thing that ruined my life? Why would anyone be a part of creating this? Don't they know what they're doing?

That night, in the car, on the way home from Utah, I discovered something about myself, and I decided to forgive—them and me—and move forward.

You see, at 8 years old, I hadn't really seen another naked body besides my own and maybe my mom or sister. Even then, I hadn't ever taken time to really observe a body until I was exposed at the sleepover. This was a big problem, because there were 3 things that I didn't know about what I had seen in the magazine.

The first is that women (and men for that matter) who model for a living are paid to keep a slender body. That is literally how they make their income. So of course they're going to take extreme measures to keep their bodies looking that way. They might do that by over-exercising, cutting calories, or skipping meals altogether.

The second thing I didn't know is the length they'll go to, in the modeling industry, to get a good shot. Deceptive lighting, angles, hair & makeup, props, and clothing (if you're lucky) are used. Not to mention the distorted and unnatural facial and body positioning. If you've ever watched an episode of America's Next Top Model, you'll know what I mean.

Finally, and I think you know where I'm headed next, I didn't know about digital alteration to photos. I'm not just talking about airbrushing or removing blemishes. I'm talking about artificially shrinking body parts down to a fraction of their original size, all with the intention of looking attractive or "beautiful". Not only do these people look like they have skin that's perfectly smooth and even toned, but they also have thin waists, curves in "all the right places", voluminous hair, long lashes, eyebrows on fleek, and legs for days. All the things that the media and big corporations want us to think are beautiful so we'll purchase what they're selling. Not only is this crazy, it's socially acceptable for most magazines, and it's completely unattainable.

In 8th grade, I used to flip through health magazines and circle the stomachs of the girls who had the kind of abs I wanted. My mom would get mad at me and try to throw them away and I didn't know why at the time. Can you see how this is so damaging? I tried exercise programs and dieting as a preteen. I even tried making myself throw up because I felt so fat. I was 13 years old.

I struggled with a very distorted body image up into my early 20s. I got married when I was 20 years old and my husband would tell me I was beautiful, but I didn't believe him. I thought that was something he had to say because he married me.

Have you been in a similar situation? We all have a vice, a destructive habit, something we want so badly to change. For me it was my body image. What is it for you? What is a trait—physical, mental, social, or emotional—that you'd like to improve? How do you get out of destructive patterns of thinking and living?

First, we must examine what's going on inside our brains.

Lets take the following scenario involving someone you deeply care about. This person has spent a few hours cleaning the kitchen and preparing a beautiful meal. You can see that this person is very tired, but proud of the work done to prepare the meal and make the environment inviting. This person, your dear, dear friend and loved one, places the meal onto a tray to carry it over to the dining table. On the way to the table you watch as this sweet friend slips and falls. The tray comes flying out of his or her hands. All the items of food fly up into the air and come pummeling to the ground. Splat. The meal is destroyed, the kitchen, a disaster.

In that instant, what do you say to this person you care so deeply about? What is your first instinct or reaction?

Now, imagine going up to this person whom you love dearly,

looking them in the face and saying, "You idiot. What have you done? What a waste. You are so clumsy. In fact, you're no good at anything. You always mess things up. Was it really that hard to move the food to the table? Why can't you do anything right?"

If what you just read shocked you, let's revisit the scenario.

This time it's YOU in the kitchen. You've spent a few hours cleaning the kitchen and preparing a gorgeous meal (if you do say so yourself). You are very tired, but you're so proud of the work you've done to prepare the meal and create an inviting environment. You carefully place the meal onto a tray and begin carrying it over to the dining room table. On the way to the table—out of nowhere—you slip. You watch helplessly as the tray, covered with all the delicious looking food, goes flying from your grasp. Then, almost in slow motion, you see it all come crashing to the ground around you.

In that instant, what do you say to YOURSELF?

Imagine if instead of self-hatred and belittling you picked yourself up and thought, "Am I hurt? How am I feeling? It's okay. Everything is going to be fine. I did such a wonderful job this morning. I am so amazing. I know I can recover from this. Sometimes things like this happen. I'll ask for some help. Let's go grab a broom and turn on some music! I have really been wanting to try that new restaurant downtown anyway. I'll take a friend and we'll laugh and cry about what happened together."

When your first internal reaction to yourself is negative, it's hard to love yourself. You must actively fill your mind with positive thoughts about you. It's not something that just magically happens.

There are 3 steps to changing the way you speak to yourself from negative to positive. The first step is becoming aware of HOW you talk to yourself. Picture a loudspeaker above your head and all of your thoughts being broadcast to those around you. What would you hear? Are those words something you'd feel comfortable saying toward another person you care about? If you're thinking "I'm too fat" or even, "I need to lose weight," imaging yourself saying to a close friend or loved one, "You are too fat. You need to lose weight." You would probably NOT say that to another human, so stop saying it to you.

The second step is to take the thoughts you recognize as negative and reframe them. Let's take the example above. "I'm too fat. I need to lose weight." You could frame this in a positive way. Try, "I am so grateful for my body because it does so many wonderful things for me. I love myself. I care so much about me that I choose to make time to show my body respect through movement and good nutrition." That may seem like a lot, and it is, but the more detailed you can get, the better. You show that negative thought who is boss and push it right on out of your mind. This happened to me today. As I write this I'm suffering from a very severe throat infection. It's painful to swallow, talk, and sometimes, it even hurts to breathe. I looked up at the clock and realized that it had been two hours past when I was supposed to take some pain medication. I thought, "Oh no! I forgot! Today is going to be a bad day." I stopped myself. I knew that if I continued to hang onto that thought, it WOULD be a bad day. So I said this to myself instead, "I choose to make today a great day. I am strong. My body is great at healing. Today will be what I create it to be."

The final step is to be gentle with yourself. At first, it might help to talk to yourself like you would talk to a child, a dear friend, or a loved one. Be your own cheerleader, supporter, encourager, and friend. Be patient because it is a daily process and there's no such thing as perfect when it comes to your thoughts. It's not possible to control them at all times. But you can be conscious and choose what thoughts to replace and what to replace them with.

Ultimately, the power to view yourself as beautiful, capable, and irreplaceable is in your control. You are beautiful. You are powerful. You are important. You are irreplaceable.

Do you believe it?

Clinton A. Young

Speaker, Author, "The Millennial Mentor"

Title of my Chapter: Finding "Flow" Again After Losing It All – Being in "Flow" on Purpose

Gallup polls report that 68% of employees in the US are totally disengaged in their work and are unhappy, working only because they have to earn money. Have you ever wondered why this is? And have you ever yearned for the opposite? A career and life of inspiration, where you are engaged and fulfilled and you feel like your life has meaning? We'll certainly get into that.

How many of you are living your life purpose and feel fulfilled and inspired in your career? If you answered yes, then this would mean you are totally in love with your career, the company culture in which you work, (or the company that you've created), and the specific tasks for which you are accountable?

How many of you are not living your life purpose and possibly even feel disempowered and resigned that you'll ever be happy in your career or find meaning in your work?

If you haven't started working yet, I'm sure you know someone close to you who is unhappy in their careers? Maybe it's your parents, your siblings, neighbors, or your close friends. And I'm sure that you want to find work that interests you, motivates you to grow, working with great leaders, and having opportunities for advancement.

Before we get started, I want to acknowledge you for taking action to read this chapter, and this book, and for taking action in your life to further distinguish what puts you in "flow". Congrats!

From my perspective, "flow" is the path of least resistance. It is that state of ease and grace where time is distorted, either coming to a seeming halt or flying by so fast because you're "in the zone". You're in "flow" when you could do what you're doing all day long and enjoy it. "Flow" gives you life and energy instead of taking it away.

I believe that if you just slowed down for a minute and really asked yourself what you truly want in life, you would arise at something like this...; to feel good about yourself on a consistent basis, to be connected to others, to be happy and fulfilled, and to be a contribution. And I feel that if we all knew it was possible for us as well, then we would do whatever needed to be done to achieve it.

Unfortunately, "flow" is a state that most people in life will never achieve on a consistent basis, not because they are incapable of it, but because they're just not aware to the fact that it exists or they don't know how to get into "flow" on purpose.

But that's NOT you. That's everyone else out there who are not reading books like this, who are not surrounding themselves with like minded people who can lift them up. I believe that it's because you are here with me now, reading this chapter, and taking in this information, that you CAN do this, and I know you are going to do whatever it takes to achieve your unique "flow" and feel amazing in the process.

And that's what this chapter is about, you achieving your unique "flow". I'm assuming that when you're done reading this and you have increased confidence that you can also get into your "flow", that you will feel happy for reading it and eager to learn more, yeah?

I just have one request. If you feel as though you are already living your ideal life, I ask that you consider that there is another level for you, and to suspend all beliefs, thoughts, judgments until you read this entire book. And if this is the first book of this kind that you are reading, I ask that you be courageous, and read on with reckless abandon and be open minded to know that a whole new world awaits you on the other side of awareness. Agreed?

I'm assuming because you're still reading that you agree and want to hear more.

This is the story of how I learned to get into "flow" on purpose. Through this story, you will learn how you can do the same.

It was the spring of 2006, only 1 year since moving from Boston to southern California, and I was on the way to having my first six-figure income year. Living two blocks from the ocean in Newport Beach, and enjoying the freedom of time flexibility that my new business offered, I was living the dream as they say. I was in a business where I was required to operate from my strengths and I was experiencing massive personal growth. I was in "flow".

I had just walked away from my "dream job" as West Coast Account Manager for the intercultural consulting division of a multinational firm and invested over $16,000 in a business because I saw an opportunity to earn more income, and create a better lifestyle of time flexibility. Most importantly, I saw an opportunity to find more alignment and "flow" in my life.

Although these two major life decisions, first to move across the country, and then to quit my dream job, were very challenging to make, I just knew deep down that they were leading me somewhere special. I'd always been someone who followed my intuition and feelings. It proved to be the most impactful decision in my life, not because of any of the money I was making, or even becoming an entrepreneur, but because it led me to my first mentor and ultimately introduced me to the world of personal development. This would positively change the course of my life forever.

Prior to this, I had been well educated with a Bachelors degree in Psychology and Masters degree in Organizational Psychology (psychology of business), but I didn't yet have the distinction of personal growth & development vs. academic education. Although I knew a lot about Psychology and the mind, I didn't yet know the value of understanding the "human condition". Heck, I hadn't even heard of that term. I certainly didn't know of the laws of the universe and how they enable one self to literally, consciously design your life. Although I'd heard my mom say it to me several times, I had no idea that I truly could "be, do, and have anything I wanted in my life". (There is an actual formula for this, and I speak about it in my book *The Power of Mentorship, The Law of Attraction special edition*. Get your free copy of my chapter entitled *The Process* here http://www.clintonayoung.com/theprocess.)

Even though I had experienced "flow" just a few years prior in graduate school, creating magic and miracles that led me to living overseas in Brazil and Singapore, and ultimately to my first dream job, I had no idea the beauty and profoundness of what occurred in my life. I had no idea that I could actually create this "flow" again, or how to do it. I thought I just got lucky.

Over the next few years, I made almost a half million dollars in my sales and marketing business, traveled around the world, and got married to my amazing wife. I was in "flow" baby. Most importantly above all of this was that I made quantum leaps in my understanding of myself and was living a lifestyle of continuous personal growth.

And then in 2009/2010, I lost it all, the properties, the income, the businesses, the credit lines; all gone. The next several years were some of the hardest years of my life, and very dark for me. I had feelings of shame, doubt, and confusion, and I was operating from an absolute survival mindset. My confidence was absolutely shattered and I didn't feel as though I could trust myself. Although luckily I never attempted it, I had contemplations of why people committed suicide. I almost lost my wife, not because of the material things that I had lost, but because I myself was lost. I was a shell of my former self.

After experiencing such success in my career, and then such failure, I was determined to create success again, however this time I sought meaning and purpose in my life and a desire for making a difference. I didn't want to settle for just any opportunity, even if I could make lots of money and have time flexibility.

When I summoned the courage to try again, I was absolutely gripped by fear of making a mistake, of making the wrong decision in my career. And I didn't feel like it was worth it to work a job that didn't inspire me and make full use of my gifts and talents. I felt it had to be perfect, and I had to be 100% clear before making my next move, and this would prove to be my downfall that would keep me stalled in this place for several years.

In those next few years, I had feelings of total disempowerment, mixed with spiritual awakening, and moments of brief clarity and inspiration. I was unemployed for over a year. Luckily, I have an amazing wife who had a business that allowed me some space to try to "find" myself again, although it put massive strain on our relationship and created resentment in our marriage that we're working through even today.

Over time however, I would need to get a job, and even with multiple degrees and years of experience, I found myself working a minimum wage job in a call center, totally depressed. I was confused because my winning formula of personal growth wasn't working, or at least not on the timeline that I wanted. I stayed committed however and used my breaks to meditate for 8 minutes 4 times a day.

During this challenging time, I exercised, meditated, took walks in nature by myself to contemplate, wrote in my journal, visualized, and read tons of books. My mentor had always taught me, and I'd found it to be true that personal growth and development was my pathway out of "ruts" in my life. (Side note: Two huge resources that I came across and use to this day are Tony Robbins Hour of Power morning practices cd, and Hal Elrod's book *The Miracle Morning*. I highly recommend picking up a copy of both.)

Then one day on my morning walk, I was contemplating the reason why I lost it all. I had made some poor decisions financially and in real estate that came back to bite me when the market shifted, and my business wasn't able to support my negative cashflow properties or my lifestyle.

I remember realizing that I felt my intuition had failed me when I bought those properties and this is why I was so perplexed and stuck, because I've always been someone who followed my intuition. I felt that if my intuition failed me, then now what do I do? I felt like a ship without a rudder.

Then all of a sudden a vision popped in my head of the day I bought the properties. I remembered that my intuition was telling me not to do it, not to buy those properties. I had allowed greed and youthful exuberance to take over and I neglected my intuition, my emotional guidance system.

In that moment I realized that it wasn't my intuition that failed me, but rather it was I who failed my intuition. This was a big shift for me, and began the process of trusting my intuition again, but it certainly didn't happen over night. Even with this new insight, I still felt lost and confused, albeit grateful for continued expansion of my awareness.

Staying committed to my self-discovery, I immersed myself back in personal development and I came across a profile tool that would prove to be the single greatest accelerator of my "flow" and clarity in my life. It was a profiling system that assessed my current level of "flow" at that time and helped me understand what puts me in my unique state of flow; what is my path of least resistance. Although we are all similar, we each have our own unique state of "flow". Now, it wasn't over night, it's definitely a commitment to a life of self-discovery. But what I found was that this profile was a huge catalyst to allow me to get back into "flow" and stay in "flow".

Since taking the profile, I've created a path back to earning six figures, I'm traveling the world again, and I'm totally inspired by what's possible in my career as The Millennial Mentor, where I help college age students discover their own unique "flow", providing them with practical tools and skills to unlock their potential and find more meaning and purpose in their life, to achieve their dream career.

I'll leave you with one final story that was truly impactful, and points to the fact that we are all products of the books we read and the people with whom we associate. (Key to success: Find a mentor and community of like-minded individuals with similar aspirations who are on the same path of personal self-discovery).

On a recent safari trip to South Africa, my mentor (who actually created the "flow" profile), shared with me something that gave me massive insight into a blind spot in my awareness that was keeping me stuck. He said that clarity does NOT precede flow. You do not get "clear", and then find your "flow". You get into your "flow" first, and in that process, you find clarity.

What I mean by that is if you think of a body of water, a pond for example. And you picture it being muddy and murky. You could say that the pond lacks clarity, right? It's stagnant. However, as you flow water through that pond, that flow of water creates movement and clarity inside of that pond. You see, "flow" actually creates clarity.

In that moment, I realized that I had been completely attached to feeling that I had to get "clear" before taking action, saying "I don't know what I want to do, I don't want to make a mistake". I was totally gripped in fear from the traumatic financial experience that I had endured and I was allowing it to keep me stuck. I was short-circuiting my own success by doubting myself and going in and out of inspiration. I discovered that I was simply not taking proper action to get back into "flow".

Continuing to immerse myself in personal growth and surrounding myself with high quality people, and ultimately learning about the "flow" profile has enabled me to vastly deepen my level of self-awareness, and it has built my confidence back to take massive action on my big vision of becoming The Millennial Mentor, helping this vibrant young generation to "Awaken to their Greatness".

Going through all of these experiences has been beautiful at times, and excruciating at others. One thing for sure is that it has lit a fire in me and uniquely prepared me for guiding young people to discover their "flow" and "path of least resistance", igniting a passion for growth, so they can unleash their potential and create their dream careers.

I've prepared a special video for the *Find Your Flow* community and a free quiz where in less than 5 minutes you will determine which of the 4 Geniuses you are and begin to discover your unique "flow". www.clintonayoung.com/findyourflow.

Interview with Jules Schroeder, Founder of CreateU

Winston: Hello and welcome to the Find Your Flow™ Radio Show podcast. I am your host, Winston Widdes, and I am here today with a *very* special guest. In fact, this is someone I have been excited to try to get a hold of and get on the show for a while now and I'm so excited she's finally here. Her name is Jules Schroeder and she's the host of "Unconventional Life", a podcast and blog that airs on the Forbes Under 30 Channel that's all about millennials that earn their living in non-traditional ways.

She actually ran her first six-figure company at the tender age of 18 and her first seven-figure company at the age of 22. She's the founder of CreateU, which is a platform in collaboration with the "People and Planet Project" of the United Nations and they are out to re-imagine higher education. She's not only doing these amazing things, she's also a very talented musician who I've had the good fortune to see first-hand. She's an artist, a performer; she's just got it going on in so many directions. She's a total badass. Please help me welcome to the show, Jules Schroeder.

Jules: Thanks so much Winston for that intro. So good to be on the show with all of your listeners.

Winston: Thank you so much. So Jules, you have so many amazing things going on. I've been reading your Forbes articles as they've been coming out and that's so cool. What kind of things are you excited about right now? What have you been up to? What are your big projects that you have going on?

Jules: Definitely a lot going on. I like to define myself as being multi-passionate and I don't think you should have to compartmentalize the things that you enjoy doing. Because, for myself, I'm multiply self-expressed in a lot of areas. So if you are listening out there and you are the same way, it's totally okay. Funny enough, I had a guy that went to my website the other day and he's like, "I hope you don't take this the wrong way, but your website is a little 'ADD'."

And, I'm like yeah, there's kind of a lot going on. You can see my YouTube videos, you can talk about the Forbes stuff, you can see CreateU, so it's a funny little bit to share. But to come back to your question, I'm super excited about this Forbes blog and my podcast, Unconventional Life. I launched that maybe two months ago, and before I launched the blog with Forbes, I would've never classified myself as a writer. My background's been in online marketing, and so I have done copywriting, but when it comes to sitting down and actually writing blogs and content, that for me was such a stretch. It was something I always wanted to do but I'm like, oh, I'm just better at speaking so I should just stick to that. And for me, I was like, how do I create a structure to hold me accountable? How do I create a game that is big enough for me to want to play so that I will consistently show up day in and day out and actually do it? And so funny enough, I said to my boyfriend literally three days before, I think I want to start writing for Forbes. And he looks at me, and he's like 'ok' and no joke, I literally look in my inbox a few days later and the Editor from the 'Under 30' channel was like, "Do you want to start writing for us?" I was like, yeah. And she asked, "How soon could you start?" And I said I'm launching this podcast. And she said, "Do you want to host it on our channel?" It was like, perfect!

And so the long and short of it is that for the last two months, I've been putting out these articles and these interviews twice a week, interviewing people from all different facets. The coolest part of what I'm doing with Unconventional Life is I'm storytelling. So, particularly those millennials—I myself am 26—those that have a story about how they're earning their living in nontraditional ways. If I can showcase more models and examples of how to get out there and do what you want, even if there isn't a path that's already been blazed or a niche carved out for your idea, that it's totally okay to go for it and so it's really fun to get in there and to make it happen.

Winston: That's so cool because I saw this post on Facebook the other day, somebody was commenting on a video about a kid doing a TEDx talk and he was talking about unfortunately schools are kind of making kids less educated. His premise was that the schools kind of put you in a box and they don't let you be creative or see outside of the box. And so for you to be doing what you are doing, highlighting people that are doing things outside the box and saying, yes, this is ok, these other people are doing it; here's some models. That's so important and valuable for other people to see, particularly millennials.

Jules: Totally. And that's exactly the premise of it: it's how do we highlight, how do we give very concrete tangible actionables? So if you are listening to the show, you can be like, "oh, I can do that right now," and implement that, even if what you're working on is totally still an idea, and so yeah, that's exactly it.

Winston: Super cool; I'm so excited to hear that. So I wanna change things up just a bit. We've got this new segment on the show; it actually starts today with you, so yay! It's kind of a format or model that I took from somebody else's podcast. I wanna ask you — one of the big things with this podcast is this idea of #socialflow, and right now I get to be social and talk to you and learn about the cool things you're doing out in the world, but I also want to know about coincidences and serendipities and luck and interactions and things that happen. I want to know about coincidences and life changing experiences that have been significant for you. Go!

Jules: Awesome question. So July last year, near death experience: wakeboarding accident, let's start there…. But to back up a minute; my life has been a series of coincidences, and I call it manifesting. All I mean by that is having a very clear thing that you are committed to and being completely unattached to the form in which it shows up. Having a specific goal like I want to start writing for Forbes and completely unattached to how that will happen and then allowing the space for it to show up. Because, in another model, I could've been like, I want to write for Forbes. Let me go out and email ten different people that write for Forbes and see if I can get an introduction. But in the model that I'm talking about, this social flow, it's being very clear in what you are committed to and unattached to the form or shape in which it manifests into you life. I wanted to highlight that for a second because it gives a little bit of precontext to last July. So, there I was, in Colorado, where I live, and I was on the water. It was a beautiful summer morning, and I jumped awake, caught an edge, face landed. I've had a history of snowboarding; and doing a lot of things like that and so I'm like, I'm kind of hurt but I think I'm going to be all right. An hour later, I got off the boat and I was in the bathroom, and all of a sudden my whole body and face started getting numb. I was barely able to get out of the stall. I got to my friend and I looked at her and said something is terribly wrong. I was having all this pain in my neck, my vision started to go out. She took me to the hospital; I don't remember much of that; got an MRI. The next thing I remember is being on the hospital bed and this white figure and six black shadow council members approached me and we had this conversation. They were like, "Jules, you have more work to do in the world. Do you want to do it?" And in that moment, I was like, yes! And my body has to work. I thought I was going to be paralyzed, so I was clear that if I was coming back, I wasn't coming back as a vegetable. After that conversation, I literally got zapped back into my body. I felt this energy forge my neck back together, shoot down my spine and it shook me. I was in the hospital for a few days, and the next brace for the following month.

But, what started happening after that accident was nothing short of serendipity. I got a phone call two weeks later from the woman that I had met six months prior at a speaker workshop. She's like "Hey, could you come do some consulting for us?" And I'm still in the neck brace and thinking in my head, is that really the best time? But there was something about that invitation that felt like a full-bodied yes. As soon as she said it, everything in my being was like, yes.... And so, I ended up going to meet her and do consulting with her and it turns out that she's working for the United Nations on the 17 global goals campaign and...she's looking for 17 ambassadors in these areas like social problems, clean water and education. And out of nowhere, what comes out of my mouth is, well, I can help you with education and I've got this thing called CreateU. Before this accident, I had no education start-up, no business, no plan, no website. It was very synergistic. And then she was like, "Can you get this running in a few weeks to present it?" I was like yeah, sure. So it was something that very divinely started coming about and I had three weeks to get my business together and that's what launched this higher education initiative....

The pieces to highlight in the flow are 1) having that accident, for me, it felt like a culmination of a chapter of how my life was before. And before, I wasn't in higher education at all. I was actually pursuing a conversation about helping musicians and the struggling artists. And there was this crazy life accident, and my life went in a complete 180. If you're listening, and you've had a crazy experience, maybe not as extreme as a near-death, but sometimes we get these things that happen, and if you are willing to pay attention to them, that's what's meant to propel you. The second thing — when I got that phone call, literally listening in my body, a full-bodied hell, yes and recognizing that once that happens, you just have to move forward with it. And that really pieced it all together and led me to ultimately getting invited to Forbes Under 30 conference in Philadelphia last November; I did a bunch of stuff with the UN and ultimately led to what I'm doing now. It was all piece after piece after piece. So, serendipitous social flow is how my life tends to pan out. And being really open and receptive to those signs when they come in. Sometimes, they are in the form of a challenging experience, like a wakeboarding accident; those are the things that are really meant to shapeshift you in the direction you're meant to go.

Winston: Whoaa, that's incredible. That's amazing. When did this happen?

Jules: This was last July. Less than a year ago; nine months ago.

Winston: If I remember, you and I met...at an event hosted by Tiamo in like April or May of last year?

Jules: Yeah.

Winston: So we met then, and I remember you obviously had your stuff together and you got a lot of experience and a lot of know-how. And I remember you talking about ending this struggling artist conversation, this kind of path and mind-set that some of these artists face. So I didn't realize the timeline here, so that's incredible; so that's how you got into...wow.

Jules: Yeah, it was literally what I was doing before. It was like okay, empowering artists and musicians. Bam! Wakeboarding accident. Jules, think much bigger. And yeah, then I did.

Winston: Wow, that's so cool. So, you've got the CreateU, you're working with the United Nations, they're kind of a big deal, right?

Jules: Yeah.

Winston: That's amazing.... What would you say to people who maybe haven't had that kind of clarity or haven't had that kind of incident? Maybe they had glimpses but they kind of write them off or they think that's too big, that's too crazy, you know, any kind of guidance? One thing you said too about your podcast that I thought was really cool was this idea of step-by-step, or like actionable steps. I think that's really important because sometimes when you're talking to somebody and they're telling you all about the great things that they're doing, and it's like, cool, I wanna do that, what do I do?...But if you're in a position like you are, where you are sharing actionable steps, what might be a step for somebody who's trying to get started or figure it out?

Jules: Well, I think the first thing is that a lot of people that I talk to that listen to the show, and some of the feedback I get is this whole self-doubt; can I do it? Will I be successful?... I just want to say that never goes away. I am still constantly having thoughts like that. The other day, I felt like my views were low on two of my posts and I was freaking out. And I ended up having this crazy dream and…in the dream, I was like casted out of my podcast post, and I wasn't able to write anymore. Everything hit the fan and I felt through all of that and I woke up and Forbes had shared the post all over social media and it ended up blowing up. It was crazy how my internal dialogue and dream was so contrasting to the external reality of what was happening. So if you are listening right now and you have any version of self-doubt or not knowing if you are the right person to deliver the thing you want to deliver into the world, the answer absolutely is yes.

And so, the first step would be knowing that if you have a vision, for anything, no matter how big or how small, there's a reason you have that vision. And no one else has the vision like you have the vision. And so if you go out there and you share it with people, and some people are super inspired…and others just don't get it, that's okay. Not everyone is going to get your vision in the right way and it's really your role to keep going and showing up and painting it for them in the world.

And so step 1 would be like just accept that your vision is your vision and you're the right one, so whatever excuses or things that are limiting you from taking that first step, acknowledge them and just keep going anyway.

Step 2 will be showing up. I think it's easy to listen to me on the show and all my successes. But on the flip side, there's been a lot of failures. And I think, only to the degree in which you are willing to be with your failures is the degree in which you are able to have success…. In my own life, I did a lot of snowboarding for a while, and I've had six concussions. The last one that I had was my senior year of graduating college in 2011 and I had really bad post-concussion syndrome from that. Literally for a year I couldn't process things in my brain. I couldn't make sense of conversation. I would have these brain fogs where it would last for hours on end and stuff would get fuzzy. Though I've healed from that, I'm not fully healed. Every day, I am fighting this, still being like a survivor of a traumatic brain injury. It's constantly in my awareness…. And so, there are a lot of circumstances that I manage behind the scenes: I've has business partners embezzle up to $200,000 worth of money, I've had clients quit, I've lost and drained all of my personal savings at different periods of time. It would've been easy in any one of those instances to say no, I think that's a sign, I'm out; I'm going to go bury my head.

…. I am sharing all of this because it is important to normal life. If you are afraid that you might fail, that's awesome. Fail fast and fail hard and do it again because that allows you to ultimately move on to the right thing. And when you finally do the right thing, it will be this internal alignment. And that's what it is for me with CreateU, with the podcast; it took a lot of the wrong things to get here, but now that I've got here, every day I wake up and it's like, yeah, that's it. There is very much a process of trusting and knowing.

So if I were break it down to recap: step 1, know you're the only one with your vision and it's your job to bring it into the world. Step 2, self-doubt and thoughts will never go away. Step 3: show up always even if you don't feel like it; show up. Your consistency in showing up is what will make the difference. Step 4, know that when the timing is right, you will soar.

Winston: That was so good. That's such an incredible story. It so cool that you share the flip side of it because it's so easy to look at the success that somebody has…. It's super-intimidating, to be honest. I can see, I mean, looking at you, you're 26, you have 6/7 figure company, you write for Forbes, you have a podcast channel, you're creating this online university with the United Nations. The reality is you have done so many things that haven't necessarily worked out the way you thought they would. You had these major circumstances in your life that you had to fight through and survive through. Sometimes people forget that at the end of the day, you're still a real person; you're not immune to life…. That's really inspiring so thank you for sharing that….

Another thing you said was…how you had this idea of wanting to write for Forbes. And you could have gone to all these writers and try to work your way in, but instead you kind of held your vision and you were open to it coming to you and showing up however it would come to you and then it did, like magic…. What other things have you done this with? How is this practice that you do in your everyday life?

Jules: I think, you know for me and for those that are listening, it's really important to figure out the thing for you. One thing that I am clear on in my life is that sitting down, writing goals and creating vision boards and having like a daily routine and daily practice, absolutely does not work for me…. I get bored if I'm forced to do the same thing every morning; that for me restricts my creativity and it drives me crazy. My boyfriend is the total opposite. He gets up every morning, goes on a 10-minute walk, makes his coffee…eats his breakfast, he meditates and then he gets ready for work. I appreciate that about him. That doesn't work for me, so…what I am going to share is what works for me. And it's important to figure out what works for you and being willing to just experiment and try…. For me what does work is paying attention to the feelings and sensations that are happening for me in the present moment. And that is the compass I use to guide what is my next direction.

For most of my life, I was pretty 'heady', I lived in my head constantly, mentally processing things…I was always on to the next thing. As a result, I really abandoned my body, what I also call the feminine side. Everyone has a feminine part of them, and for a long time, being hyper-driven, I was very much in my masculine and ignoring this feminine flowness, checking-in space. And I think that the access to manifesting or finding a social flow or having these things appear is stepping into that feminine, whether you are a guy or whether you are a girl; that it's in the slowness that actually gives enough space for things to show up in the way that they're meant to. A practice that you can do right now is noticing your internal compass. And if you're someone like who I was…in your head a lot, it's just 'dropping' back into your body. And that might start with pausing and taking a few breaths and just slowing the noise for two seconds. And then building it into something concrete, paying attention to what experience you have when you're faced with a choice…. If it's an instant 'hell yes', then it's a yes. But if it's a maybe, or you're not sure, then it's just a 'no'. If you stop paying attention to 'maybe' and being on the fence and being unsure and just go for those 'hell yeses', that will instantly drive you in the right direction for these bigger opportunities…in your own life to show up…. I started doing this practice two years ago and since I've done that, everything that has appeared in my life has been more intentional and more aligned with things that I actually want…. It feels good because every time you say no, you're making room for an even bigger yes….

Winston: Wow, that was amazing; I loved that. There are a couple of things that I wanna touch back on.... You were talking about the female energy and the male energy. I really resonated with that because I'm also or have been a very 'heady' person as you described...and then the experience I had recently was I kind of was forced out of my mind and into more of a let's open space up for how things might show up differently than what I'm trying to hold on to. That was when, as you described it, I was more in my feminine energy and more space and body and open and that's when things started rushing in; all these opportunities that I had been chasing, showed up. They weren't exactly how I thought they would be, but they were calling me and landing in my lap instead of me going out and chasing.... It's so insightful and super fantastic. Thank you so much for saying all that.

Jules: Yeah, to get even a step further on it, there's this thing called human design. You can go to jovianarchives.org and actually find your human design, your blueprint.... The premise is that we all have this blueprint of how we operate. And when we are in line with that blueprint, it gives us the way in which we should respond to things that are happening in our life. For me, I'm what human design calls a manifesting generator. I find the best source of my power when I'm being called on, and when I'm responding. So when I'm proactively going to do stuff, I'm getting no results, but when I'm waiting and responding to things that are coming to me, that's my most powerful source to show up.... Getting more into the human design work could be a cool place to start for your own way of how to navigate through some stuff.

Winston: I'm so happy you shared all these amazing things, Jules and I know there are people out there that are going to want to follow you and know what you're up to.... Where can people listen to your podcasts, where can they find your articles on Forbes? Can you share some of those resources for us, please?

Jules: You can go to iTunes to check out my podcast Unconventional Life.... You can also go to Forbes and just search Jules Schroeder and you can go to my personal website, JulesSchroeder.com. And every week on the podcast, we are giving away actionable resources like free courses and books and stuff from the guests. So if you want to enter for one of those giveaways, it's totally free to enter. It's www.UnconventionalLifeShow.com and you can win some cool actionable tools to get started on whatever you're working on in your own life.

Winston: ...So Jules, thank you so much for being on the show today. I really appreciate it. I got a ton out of it; I'm sure our listeners did too. Any final words or thoughts that you want to share?

Jules: Thanks so much for having me and the last thing I want to say is just go for it. If you're sitting there and you're listening and there's something percolating, whatever it is, just get out there and do it and see what happens.

Winston: Well said! Well said! And this is from somebody that's gone out and done it and is doing it right now. Congratulations on all your awesome things, I'm just so excited for you, and all the amazing things you're doing and doing for the world, because this is stuff that I think is really important for people to be made aware of and to have something to look up to and see these models and see actionable steps and be able to use it in their own lives. Thank you for the work that you're doing.

Jules: Thank you so much, Winston.

In Conclusion

I feel so happy to be able to bring together such fascinating and flowing people!

Flow told me about her contact improvisation and I could really sense her passion for it and told her it reminded me of how I feel about jiu-jitsu. You can learn more about her amazing work at http://www.embodiedevo.com

Ashley's story is such an important message and she is so talented and loving and awesome. It's so cool to listen to her music and see her perform as a singer-songwriter. You can check her out at www.AshleyLudlow.com

No Pants Sammi is no joke. I recently watched some videos of her lifting at a competition...UNREAL. Keep an eye on her at www.NoPantsSammi.com Listen to her podcast interview: http://findyourflow.com/podcast/no-pants-sammi/

I got inspired by Clinton's "flow personality test" because when he did one on me I really was blown away. I actually feel like it is quite amazing and I can't wait for him to share it with the world. Oh, I guess we are doing that right now. Sharing it that is. In this very book. Thank YOU, by the way, for reading it and buying it with your money. I appreciate the support. :) Now go there and get yourself some flow insights like you've never experienced before! www.clintonayoung.com/findyourflow

Speaking with Jules was pretty fantastic. She almost died, then came back with a whole new life mission. It gave me chills. You can hear the interview at: http://findyourflow.com/podcast/find-your-flow-podcast-18-jules-schroeder-mindflow/

Check out her podcast for Forbes at:

www.UnconventionalLifeShow.com

Hopefully you experienced some more flow for yourself. Thank you for reading stuff like this. Its good for humanity. :)

Until next time my friend...be flowing.

--Winston

www.ingramcontent.com/pod-product-compliance
Lightning Source LLC
Chambersburg PA
CBHW030037230526
45472CB00002B/556